STANDARDIZED TESTING IN SCHOOLS

STANDARDIZED TESTING IN SCHOOLS

BY HOLLY DOLEZALEK

Content Consultant
Robyn Lea' Sayre, Educator/English
BA, MAEd Georgian Court University, NJ

ABDO
Publishing Company

CREDITS

Editor: Jill Sherman
Copy Editor: Patricia Stockland
Interior Design and Production: Nicole Brecke
Cover Design: Nicole Brecke

Library of Congress Cataloging-in-Publication Data

Dolezalek, Holly.
  Standardized testing in schools / by Holly Dolezalek.
      p. cm. — (Essential viewpoints)
  Includes bibliographical references and index.
  ISBN 978-1-60453-113-8
  1. Educational tests and measurements—United States. I. Title.

LB3051.D64 2009
371.26'2—dc22

                                2008011897

TABLE OF CONTENTS

U.S. President Ronald Reagan mandated educational reform in the 1980s.

No Child Left Behind

or many years, U.S. citizens have been concerned about the state of public education. In 1983, the Department of Education commissioned a report on the subject. That report, titled "A Nation at Risk," said that test scores in the

United States had declined in the 1960s and 1970s. The report called for U.S. public schools to be reformed.

Since that report was published, even more attention has focused on school reform. Lawmakers look at test scores to determine whether schools are improving. At the time of the report, President Ronald Reagan wanted to scale back the federal role in public education. Every president since Reagan, however, has been committed to improving public education through more federal involvement.

The Elementary and Secondary Education Act (ESEA) established federal funding for all schools. In 1993 and 1994 this act was up for reauthorization. Many legislators wanted to add the concept of "accountability" to the act. They wanted to require public schools both to educate students and to show that students were being educated. Prior to this act, standardized tests generally showed how well all students nationwide were learning. But under new legislation, standardized tests would be required so that each school could show how successful it had been in improving students' knowledge.

The No Child Left Behind (NCLB) Act passed Congress in 2001. President George W. Bush signed it into law on January 8, 2002. The act's goal is to make sure that every student is proficient in reading and math by 2014.

NCLB is a controversial act. Teachers, educators, parents, and lawmakers have all weighed in on the debate. Some feel that the act is invasive. They feel that standardized testing takes away from time in the classroom. Others want to see schools held accountable for their progress. They feel that standardized tests are the best way to measure student progress.

NCLB Testing Requirements

NCLB required that by the 2005–2006 school year, all students between third and eighth grade had to be tested annually in reading and mathematics. It also required all students to be tested at least once during tenth, eleventh, or twelfth grade in reading and math.

The Purpose of No Child Left Behind

According to the Statement of Purpose in the No Child Left Behind Act of 2001, "The purpose of this title is to ensure that all children have a fair, equal, and significant opportunity to obtain a high-quality education and reach, at a minimum, proficiency on challenging State academic achievement standards and state academic assessments."[1]

President George W. Bush signed NCLB legislation in 2002.

Beginning in the 2007–2008 school year, the act required that students also be tested in science three times: once each during grades three through five, six through nine, and ten through twelve.

All of these tests must be standardized. The only exception is if a state chooses to use local tests in different districts. The local tests have to be similar to each other. They must be equally difficult no matter which district a student takes the test in.

Prior to 1994, when ESEA was last reauthorized, schools had only been required to test their students in grades three through five. Under the new law, schools must test in seven grades. NCLB doubled the required amount of testing. NCLB requires this expansion of testing to make schools more accountable for their students' progress.

Schools that receive federal funding must conduct these tests and meet other requirements of the act. For instance, as of the 2005–2006 school year, all

Funding NCLB

Several lawsuits have been filed since NCLB was signed into law. These suits allege that while NCLB is well intentioned, it is underfunded. Although the law requires school districts and states to take certain actions, the federal government does not provide funds so that they can do so. The act states:

Nothing in this Act shall be construed to authorize an officer or employee of the Federal Government to mandate, direct, or control a State, local education agency, or school's curriculum, program of instruction, or allocation of State or local resources, or mandate a State or any subdivision thereof to spend any funds or incur any costs not paid for under this Act. [2]

Based on this provision, school districts in Michigan, Texas, and Vermont, and the National Education Association (NEA) sued the Department of Education. They said that they were not getting the funds they needed to comply with NCLB.

On January 8, 2008, the U.S. Court of Appeals for the Sixth Circuit ruled that because states must comply with NCLB regardless of federal funding, NCLB violated the Constitution.

The Department of Education may appeal that decision. But in the meantime, states will no longer have to comply with provisions of NCLB that they do not have funds for.

public school teachers are required to be "highly qualified." That means that teachers must have a bachelor's degree and must have "proven knowledge" of the subjects that they teach. They also must be licensed to teach in the state where they teach.

Adequate Yearly Progress

Another important requirement of NCLB is adequate yearly progress, or AYP. This is a measured improvement in students' test scores. Each school must show AYP every year. Schools also must show that at least 95 percent of all students in each required grade took the state's test.

Each state sets its own goals for its AYP. But if a school fails to meet its goals for two years in a row, students at that school have the option to transfer to another public school in that district. Schools that do not show AYP for two straight years are designated as "failing." These schools must offer students tutoring or other supplemental educational services.

Each state is responsible for determining which tests to use for each subject, and how the tests will measure the AYP goals. All AYP goals must contribute toward achieving the final NCLB goal: 100 percent proficiency by the year 2014.

CONTROVERSIAL ACT

NCLB has been controversial since the day it was passed. Its requirements are difficult. Supporters of the legislation argue that the requirements should be difficult. Previous versions of ESEA sought to improve public education by encouraging states to adopt ambitious AYP goals. However, supporters of NCLB say that it was easy for schools to avoid making significant changes. According to author W. James Popham:

> [B]ecause educational policy makers in most states were reluctant to set particularly demanding AYP expectations for their state (fearing that many of the state's schools might be unable to meet those expectations), a number of states established AYP targets that were absolutely trifling.[3]

NCLB, on the other hand, makes it very difficult for any school to do that.

Opponents object to NCLB for many reasons. Whether it is the AYP requirements, the criteria for teachers to be "highly qualified," or other provisions of the act, opposition to NCLB has been intense. In fact, legislatures in several states, including Arizona, Hawaii, New Mexico, Utah, Vermont, and Virginia, have voted not to comply with part or all of the law.

Since 2004, more than 140 educational organizations have signed a Joint Organizational Statement that recommends many changes in the law. Some of these organizations include the American Association of School Administrators, the American Federation of Teachers, and the National Education Association.

Opposition to NCLB comes from a very simple but deep disagreement: that the act relies too heavily on standardized testing. Students' scores have big consequences for the schools. But do good test scores really mean better education? Supporters of NCLB, particularly the Department of Education under the Bush administration, argue that test scores hold teachers and schools accountable. They say test scores show whether schools are providing a good education to their students.

The law's many opponents say that test scores do not equal good

Supplemental Educational Services

Supplemental educational services provide extra help for students. If a student is attending a school that has been designated as "failing," that student is entitled under NCLB to get tutoring or other extra help in his or her classes. Each state education agency makes a list of organizations that can provide this help. The services are paid for by the school. The student can get help either before or after school, on weekends, or during the summer.

education. Many educators find it difficult to motivate students to perform well on standardized tests. Such tests do not always directly affect the students' grades. In addition, under NCLB students and parents are not held accountable for the students' performance. Opponents of the law also say that the penalties for poor test scores do not help "failing" schools to improve. Critics argue that 100 percent proficiency is not a reasonable goal for all children at the same time and in the same time frame. ⌐

Strengthening No Child Left Behind

NCLB is up for reevaluation in 2008. Congress will have to consider President Bush's recommendations to strengthen the act. These include:

• Allowing states and districts more flexibility in implementing programs to turn around struggling schools.

• Allowing students to transfer out of low-performing school districts and receive tutoring.

• Aiding students and schools with federally funded tutoring.

• Rewarding teachers for good performance in low-income schools.

• Preparing students for college and strengthening math and science education.

NCLB mandated standardized testing across the United States.

A student takes the Illinois Standard Achievement Exam.

TESTING CONTROVERSY

*S*tudents are tested in classrooms across the United States. Students in all states take tests to show how well they have learned what they have been taught. Tests are a well-established part of teaching and education.

Standardized testing is different. Ordinary classroom tests show whether each individual student has learned specific concepts and skills. Classroom tests usually affect a student's grade in a class. Standardized tests are not used to determine grades. Standardized tests are often used to show how well all the students who take the test are learning. The scores on these tests are often used for research purposes. Administrators look at the scores to help them decide if a school is performing well and meeting its goals.

Standardized tests can be used to assess many things: personality, career interest, attitudes, aptitude, and achievement. The tests that are used in public schools are usually achievement tests. These tests measure what test takers know.

Standardized testing in schools is a very controversial subject. Teachers, parents, and researchers often disagree about whether a standardized test can truly show if students are learning.

Common Standardized Tests

- Florida Comprehensive Assessment Test (FCAT)
- Arizona Instrument to Measure Standards (AIMS)
- Connecticut Academic Performance Test (CAPT)
- Massachusetts Comprehensive Assessment System (MCAS)
- Iowa Tests of Basic Skills (ITBS)
- Metropolitan Achievement Tests (MAT)
- Basic Achievement Skills Inventory (BASI)

Why So Controversial?

It may sound strange that something as common as a test could be the cause of so much disagreement. But some important decisions are made based on the results of standardized tests. Sometimes students are held back or have to get extra tutoring when they fail a certain test. Other students may receive honors or be placed in advanced classes when they do well. Some tests affect the school and how much funding the school will receive.

One controversy with standardized tests is that many factors can affect the results. For example, the reliability of the test results is determined by how well the test was written. If the questions on a test are written properly, so that they are not confusing or unclear, the results should accurately show what the student knows. But questions on a test can be poorly written. The answer may be unclear or the question may have more than one correct answer.

Tests can also be scored in different ways depending on the test scorer. This is especially true in the case of written-response questions. Standardized tests should be graded the same way for all students. But different test scorers might award the same written response a different score. Unless all the items are multiple-choice (with only one possible answer), scoring is imperfect.

The most popular items to include on a standardized test are multiple-choice questions. But organizations such as the National Center for Fair and Open Testing argue that multiple-choice questions are not very helpful with all kinds of knowledge. "Standardized tests are tests on which all students answer the same questions, usually in multiple-choice format, and each question has only one correct answer," says a fact sheet on the

California state superintendent of public instruction Jack O'Connell announced improved scores on standardized tests in 2006.

organization's Web site. "They reward the ability to quickly answer superficial questions that do not require real thought. They do not measure the ability to think or create in any field."[3] Unless students have been taught the material that test questions ask about, they will not do well on the test.

In addition, even if a test is standardized, students' performance on the test is affected by more than what they know. While the test is the same for every student who takes it, not all students are the same. Some students have test anxiety, which means that they get very nervous about taking tests. Students with test anxiety rarely do well on a test, even if they know the material. Other students have certain learning disabilities that make tests very difficult for them. In addition, not all students speak English as their first language. If a student has trouble with English, that student may not do as well on the test no matter what he or she knows.

Opponents of standardized testing believe that "their use encourages a narrowed curriculum [and] outdated methods of instruction."[4] Further, minority, disadvantaged, and disabled students often do less well on the tests than middle-class white children.

High-stakes Testing

Since the 1980s, concern about student achievement in public schools has increased. Supporters of standardized testing say that by requiring more testing of public schools, those schools will be forced to account for how well they teach their students. Schools will have to make changes if test scores do not reflect good instruction. Many conservatives have embraced testing as a way to improve students' achievement. However, teachers' unions, such as the National Education Association and the American Federation of Teachers, have not.

Standardized testing is drawing more fire than ever because of the way it is being used under NCLB. Students are taking more tests than ever. Before NCLB was passed, standardized testing often did not affect students' lives directly. The scores were used to improve instruction. Individual students rarely suffered if they did poorly on the tests. But some standardized tests are known as high-stakes tests. A student's score on these tests has consequences for that student. For example, in order to graduate, high school students in Minnesota must pass the Graduation-Required Assessment for Diploma (GRAD) test. This is one of the many tests that are a part of NCLB assessment. The test covers reading, writing, and mathematics. This is a high-stakes test because, although a student who fails the test can take it again, that student cannot graduate or get a diploma without passing the test.

This type of high-stakes testing has been in use prior to NCLB. But today, under NCLB, the stakes are even higher. Schools with poor student test scores can lose students, be denied federal funding, or even be closed down. ⌐

*High-stakes testing seeks to make students
and teachers accountable for test scores.*

Fourth graders taking an intelligence test in 1948

THE HISTORY OF TESTING

lthough standardized testing is a modern practice, testing has been used for thousands of years. A system for testing Chinese youth existed as far back as 2200 BCE. Chinese students studied for a series of literary exams, which determined their status in Chinese society. These tests required them to write essays and poems in specific formats. They also had to demonstrate their knowledge of Confucian thought. Periodically, officials in China had to pass tests to show that they were still qualified to serve in the Chinese government.

Tests have long been a staple of university life as well. Universities began to form in the eleventh and twelfth centuries in England, France, Italy, and Spain. Students had to pass exams to graduate and earn advanced degrees. "These earliest examinations were oral, a tradition that persists to this time in doctoral programs at nearly every university," writes author James Wardrop.[1]

CREATING THE TESTS

A French psychologist named Alfred Binet was a pioneer in the use of standardized testing. Binet worked as a researcher at the Laboratory of Experimental Psychology at the Sorbonne in Paris. In 1905 he worked with Theodore Simon to create the Binet-Simon Scale. The Binet-Simon test was an intelligence quotient (IQ) test. This scale helped testers to determine whether a child was "normal" or "retarded." Children were observed while they performed increasingly complex tasks. The scale determined the child's "mental age" based on how well he or she could repeat back numbers, construct sentences, and do other tasks.

The next year, psychologist Lewis Terman revised Binet and Simon's scale and renamed it:

> *The new Stanford-Binet scale . . . would allow for the scientific diagnosis and classification of children to be placed in special classes; bring tens of thousands of high-grade defectives under the surveillance and protection of society; reduce delinquency; help the schools respond to children of superior intelligence; assist in assigning children to school grades; help determine vocational fitness; and serve as a standard for research.[2]*

TESTING GROWS IN POPULARITY

IQ testing had been gaining in popularity since the creation of the Stanford-Binet. The U.S. Army had been using its version of an IQ test to screen new recruits, and Terman had created an IQ test for elementary school children. A psychology professor named Carl Brigham had become interested in IQ testing as a way to protect the military and economic

Army recruits taking an intelligence test in 1917

superiority of the United States. He shaped the U.S. Army's IQ test into one of the most used standardized tests today, the Scholastic Assessment Test (SAT).

The first state testing program was the Iowa Every-Pupil Testing Program, which began in the early 1930s. The program began as an academic meet, sometimes called a "brain derby." It was a contest that was intended to reward good students the same way that athletic students were rewarded.

Seeing Iowa's success and desiring their own improvements, other states began to use Iowa's tests in their own testing programs. By 1940, students nationwide were taking the test.

In 1936, IBM demonstrated a machine that could score tests automatically. This machine made large-scale standardized testing more practical. Large numbers of students could take an exam consisting of multiple-choice questions. The machine could calculate all their scores correctly within a relatively short period of time.

In 1947, the Educational Testing Service (ETS) was formed. ETS, a nonprofit, would administer tests to determine which students should be admitted to higher learning or get scholarships. In 1959, American College Testing, Inc. was founded as a rival to ETS. Its standardized test was the American College Test (ACT). Today, the ACT and the SAT

ETS Criticized

ETS was formed in 1947 and has administered the SAT ever since. Not everyone was a fan of ETS. A physicist and mathematician named Banesh Hoffmann wrote *The Tyranny of Testing* in 1962. The book brought his criticisms of standardized testing to the attention of the public. As of 2008, the book was still in print and is considered a classic discussion of the flaws of standardized testing.

are among the best-known standardized tests in the United States. These tests are used solely as college entrance exams. Students take the ACT and the SAT voluntarily in order to apply to colleges.

LAWMAKERS STEP IN

In the 1970s and 1980s, the public education system in the United States came under fire. Businesses were complaining that college graduates were not prepared for the working world. College professors, in turn, suggested that high school graduates were not prepared for higher education. In 1983, the National Commission on Excellence in Education issued its "A Nation At Risk" report. The report said that SAT scores for American schoolchildren had dropped steadily from 1963 to 1980. The average verbal scores were 50 points lower than they had been in 1963. Math scores had also dropped 40 percent. "Average achievement of most high school students on most standardized tests is now lower than 26 years ago," the report said.[3] In 1989, the National Academy of Sciences issued a report on mathematics teaching in the United States. It said that the way mathematics was taught in the United States was "totally inadequate."[4]

Education in the United States became an important issue to many Americans and lawmakers. In response, budgets for education swelled, reforms took place, and more attention was paid to test scores and education in school.

Finally, a major reform took place: standards-based education. According to author John Jennings:

> *During the late 1980s, a movement began with the stated purpose of helping teachers know what they are to teach and helping students know what they are expected to learn. . . . This major change is generally labeled "standards-based" reform. It means that agreement will be achieved first on what students are to know and be able to do—the standards. Then progress through school and graduation from high school will be determined according to mastery of this content.*[5]

During the presidency of George H. W. Bush, a new education plan called America 2000 called for "standards for what children should know and be able to do in five core subjects: English, mathematics, science, history, and geography."[6] It also called for tests at fourth, eighth, and twelfth grade to help show that students were learning what they were supposed to. The plan also called for school choice, in which the federal government would help pay for students to attend private schools. Educational organizations such as the American Federation of Teachers opposed this aspect of the plan. So did some conservatives, who did not want the federal government to expand its role in education.

When President Clinton was elected in 1992, the plan was revived with some changes. The Goals 2000 legislation was introduced. Unlike America 2000, Goals 2000 passed Congress. The Goals 2000: Educate America Act of 1994 contained ideas about education standards and about testing in

America 2000

The Goals of President George H. W. Bush's education plan were as follows:

"1. All children in America will start school ready to learn.

2. The high school graduation rate will increase to at least 90 percent.

3. American students will leave grades four, eight, and twelve having demonstrated competency in challenging subject matter including English, mathematics, science, history, and geography; and every school in America will ensure that all students learn to use their minds well, so they may be prepared for responsible citizenship, further learning, and productive employment in our modern economy.

4. U.S. students will be first in the world in science and mathematics achievement.

5. Every adult American will be literate and will possess the knowledge and skills necessary to compete in a global economy and exercise the rights and responsibilities of citizenship.

6. Every school in America will be free of drugs and violence and will offer a disciplined environment conducive to learning."[7]

certain grades and subjects. These points became part of the No Child Left Behind Act (NCLB).

In the same year, Congress renewed the Elementary and Secondary Education Act (ESEA). It also made some significant changes to the ESEA that factored into the creation of NCLB.

By 2001, many Americans were still dissatisfied with the progress of reform in public education. They felt that it was time to hold schools accountable for the successes or failures of their students. On January 8, 2002, NCLB became law. It effectively doubled the amount of testing required in public education. —

Goals 2000: The Educate America Act

Most of the education goals in Goals 2000 were the same as those in the America 2000 Education Strategy. But the new legislation added two new goals:

Goal 4: By the year 2000, the nation's teaching force will have access to programs for the continued improvement of their professional skills to instruct and prepare all American students for the next century.

Goal 8: By the year 2000, every school will promote parental involvement and participation in promoting the social, emotional, and academic growth of children.

In 1992, President Bill Clinton signed Goals 2000 legislation to improve education standards.

Standardized tests in a staging area in Iowa City

STANDARDS AND SCORING

Two important aspects of standardized
tests are standards and scoring. Standards
determine how tests are created. Scoring, on the
other hand, determines how the performance of test
takers is interpreted once the test has been taken.

The two might sound simple. But standards must take many aspects of the curriculum and test development into consideration. And scoring is much more complex than whether a student gets a given question right or wrong.

STANDARDS

When a standardized test is written, the test developer starts with the curriculum objectives. For example, a test on fourth grade mathematics will not be fair unless it asks questions about the concepts of mathematics that have already been taught. The test is written based on those curriculum objectives. Then it will be tried out on fourth graders so that the developers know if any items need rewriting. It can take as long as two to three years for a test publisher to prepare and publish a standardized test.

Part of the reason that it takes so long is that test makers are often trying to comply with testing standards. The American Educational Research Association (AERA), the American Psychological

Aligning Tests with Standards

For a test to be effective it must align with whatever standards the school, state, or district has set. In other words, the test must ask questions about content that matches up with the curriculum standards. These standards are a guide for teachers, so they know what students need to be taught in each subject and in each grade.

Association (APA), and the National Council on Measurement in Education (NCME) have developed standards for good educational tests. These organizations have issued standards for educational and psychological tests.

Test standards cover all aspects of a test. One part of the standards covers how the test is written. Standards require the test to be reliable, valid, and have minimal errors of measurement. Standards also include guides for how tests should be revised and scored. They indicate the test's scales and norms. They say whether the scores should be compared to other test scores. Finally, they establish guidelines for how tests should be administered, and how test data should be reported.

Another part covers fairness in testing. It explains the rights and responsibilities of test takers. Test takers have the right to take tests that meet professional standards. Fairness standards also explain how students with disabilities or ESL students should be tested.

Finally, the standards explain how tests should be used. This covers how testing in different areas— employment, psychology, and education—is properly used.

Also, each state sets its own curriculum standards. They describe what students at each grade level should be taught. The tests attempt to measure whether students have learned the curriculum. Tests are carefully written to reflect the standards.

NORM-REFERENCED SCORES

One common method of scoring standardized tests is norm-referenced scoring. A norm-referenced test is scored based on a norm, or a group of test takers. When the test is being developed, it is administered to a group of people who are similar to the students who will ultimately take the test. For example, a test intended for fifth graders will be normed to a group of fifth graders who take the test before it is administered in a school.

Test developers carefully choose the norm group. A norm group has to be three things. "To be appropriate, a norm group must be recent,

Professional and Technical Standards

Under No Child Left Behind (NCLB), states are allowed to decide which tests to use for their standardized testing. But the act requires states to use tests that are developed according to professional and technical standards of test making. The APA, the AERA, and the NCME issued these standards in 1985 and revised them in 1999.

Grading Rubric

Scoring Trait	Did Not Meet	Meets	Exceeds
Sentences	2 or more construction errors; simple sentence structure	Minimal variety in structure; 1 construction error	Mature variety in structure; minimal errors
Punctuation	More than 3 mistakes in punctuation; comma, apostrophe, etc.	3 or fewer mistakes in punctuation; comma, apostrophe, etc.	Correct punctuation; comma, apostrophe, semi-colons, etc.

Grading rubrics such as these are used to score standardized tests.[2]

representative, and relevant," according to education specialists William Mehrens and Irvin Lehmann.[1]

To be recent, a norm group must have been tested recently. A fifth grader from 1985 may have been able to answer a question that mentioned a record player. But fifth graders today would probably be better able to answer the question if it mentioned an MP3 player. The norm group should also have similar experiences to the potential test takers. Otherwise, the comparison would be invalid, or at least not very meaningful.

To be representative, the norm group must be similar to the test takers. They should have similar ages, backgrounds, economic status, and race to the potential test takers. For instance, a student from a wealthy family would have access to things that a student from a low-income family would not. If the norm group was made up only of wealthy students, it would not be representative of all students taking the test.

Finally, to be relevant, the norm group must resemble the test takers. "If . . . a tester wishes to compare a student's ability with that of students who intend to go to college, then the norm group should be a sample of students who wish to go to college," Mehrens and Lehmann wrote.[3]

When students take the test and it is finally scored, those scores will be compared to the scores of the norm group. If a student's score is higher than the norm group's, it is a high score. If a score is similar to the norm group's score, it is average.

CRITERION-REFERENCED SCORES

Another type of scoring is criterion-referenced scoring. Scores on criterion-referenced tests are not compared to a norm group. Instead scores are

Norm- or Criterion-referenced?

The Michigan Educational Assessment Program (MEAP) is an example of a criterion-referenced test. This test is given to Michigan students at many grade levels. Michigan educators set the standards for performance on the test, and the Michigan State Board of Education approves them. Student performance on the test is then judged by those standards.

The Iowa Tests of Basic Skills (ITBS), on the other hand, are norm-referenced tests. Iowa students in kindergarten through eighth grade take the ITBS in almost all school districts. A student's Iowa percentile rank compares the students' scores to others in their grade in Iowa. The student's national percentile rank compares the scores nationally.

compared only to the test takers' mastery of the subject matter.

If a student takes a criterion-referenced test, his or her score is compared to how many items were on the test. For example, if a student gets 70 percent of the items right, his or her score is 70 percent.

The major types of criterion-referenced scores are percent-correct scores and "mastery or nonmastery" scores. A committee of experts on testing and education determines the passing, or mastery, score. If a student exceeds that score, he or she has mastered the material on the test. If a student does not exceed the score, he or she has not mastered the material. Neither norm-referenced nor criterion-referenced scores are better or more meaningful. But both have their limitations. ⌒

Multiple-choice exams help ensure that there is little error in scoring.

Standardized tests must be administered the same way for every student.

WHAT IS A
STANDARDIZED TEST?

A test must have certain characteristics in order for it to be a true standardized test. Standardized tests are developed according to accepted standards of test development. Everyone who takes the test gets the same set of questions.

They also take the test under the same conditions. They get the same instructions and have the same amount of time to finish the test. The method of scoring the test is also the same. Because these tests are a lot of work to create, standardized tests are usually developed by test-publishing companies.

Standardized tests can be delivered in a group setting or in a face-to-face setting. Most standardized tests in education are delivered in group settings. Usually, standardized tests are administered in public schools. The Iowa Tests of Basic Skills is delivered this way. However, some tests are delivered face-to-face, with one test taker and one administrator.

DIAGNOSTIC TESTS

Diagnostic tests are typically administered face-to-face. These tests are given to students who are

Test Publishers

There are several test publishers in the United States that publish standardized tests.
Riverside Publishing:
- Iowa Tests of Basic Skills

Educational Testing Service:
- Scholastic Achievement Test (SAT)
- Graduate Record Examinations (GRE)

Scholastic Testing Service:
- High School Placement Test (HSPT)

American College Testing:
- American College Test (ACT)

struggling in a particular subject. They are not given to all students, as other types of standardized tests are. But like other standardized tests, the conditions in which diagnostic tests are given are uniform, and they are scored objectively.

One example of a diagnostic test is the Gates-McKillop Reading Diagnostic Test. Students who are having trouble reading are asked to read aloud, identify words and vowel and letter sounds, answer questions about word parts, and other tasks. This helps the tester to find out which aspects of reading the student is having trouble with.

Survey Batteries

Survey batteries are standardized tests that cover

Sample Questions from the Michigan Educational Assessment Program

Multiple-Choice Question:

Which core democratic value was violated when the Supreme Court ruled in 1857 that enslaved people are not citizens?

A Truth
B Equality
C Rule of Law
D Pursuit of Happiness

Essay Question:

You will now take a stand on the public policy issue: "Should the United States government require all motorcycle riders to wear helmets?"

You may either support or oppose a United States government proposal to require all motorcycle riders to wear helmets. Write a letter to your state representative explaining your position on the issue.

many subjects and that give both overall scores and individual scores in each area. An example of a well-known survey battery is the Iowa Tests of Basic Skills (ITBS) test battery. The ITBS includes tests in reading, vocabulary, word analysis, listening, reading comprehension, language, math, social studies, science, and sources of information.

When students take battery tests, their answers show how much they know in individual subjects and what their abilities are. These tests often do not cover a state's complete curriculum. They are meant to assess general strengths and weaknesses. Teachers can then use that data in deciding what to teach, how to teach it, and what to adapt for certain students in certain areas.

READING-READINESS TESTS

Children in kindergarten and first grade often take reading-readiness

Standardized Tests and Classroom Tests: What Is the Difference?

Standardized Tests
• Developed by test-publishing companies
• Conducted in consistent conditions
• Scores are compared to a norm group
• Instructions are consistent and carefully delineated
• Intended to assess general knowledge

Classroom Tests
• Developed by teachers or textbook publishers
• Not necessarily conducted in consistent conditions
• Scores are not compared to any group
• Usually conducted by one teacher; no need for delineated instructions
• Intended to assess specific curriculum objectives

tests so that school officials will know whether they are prepared to start reading. When they take the tests, such as the Metropolitan Readiness Test, children perform tasks that show whether they have the basic skills that are important for reading. They draw, explain the definitions of words, listen to instructions, and find similar pictures or words.

However, children in this age group develop very quickly. Children who perform poorly on a test such as this may not be very far behind their better-performing peers.

COLLEGE ENTRANCE EXAMS

A well-known college entrance exam is the SAT. The SAT is a multiple-choice test of math and verbal skills. In 2005 an essay portion was added to the exam and it was renamed the SAT Reasoning Test. High school students across the country take the SAT. Every test taker

Types of Questions

• Multiple choice: A question for which test takers must choose the correct answer from several answers.
• Constructed response: A question for which test takers must write a short answer based on a map, graph, or other visual.
• Essay: A question that requires an answer in the form of an essay.
• True or false: A question for which test takers must determine whether a statement is true or false.

Wylie Mitchell of Bates College no longer looks at standardized test scores as part of the admissions process.

gets the same questions. The test administrators follow a standard set of instructions that are often read aloud. The administrators give the test takers the same amount of time to complete the test. The College Board grades all completed tests according to the standards that the board has set.

Many colleges and universities in the United States look at a student's SAT scores when considering him or her for admission. However,

some college admissions boards have begun
to question whether these tests are useful in
determining which students to accept. These schools
may not rely heavily on the scores when determining
whom to accept. SAT scores are also used by some
organizations when awarding scholarships. ⌐

Standardized tests help educators identify weaknesses in curricula.

In California, 42 percent of students scored at a proficient or advanced level on their 2006 exams.

Writing a Good Test

standardized tests are expensive. A lot of
work and time goes into each stage of
creating a standardized test. Classroom tests are
usually written by teachers or textbook publishing
companies. Classroom tests are typically scored by

the teachers who administer the tests. Teacher-made tests take a few weeks to create. Tests made by textbook companies could take months to make. But standardized tests sometimes take years to create. Standardized tests are written, tested, rewritten, normed, and interpreted by subject matter and testing experts at test-publishing companies. This does not mean that teachers are not subject-matter experts in their fields. On the contrary, many scorers for standardized tests are teachers.

DEVELOPMENT

The first decision test writers must make is what the test will measure. They must consider what subjects the test will cover, what grade level of students will take the test, what skills the test will measure, and how to measure these skills. These factors and many more are important in deciding what kinds of questions to ask, how to ask them, how to score them, and how to interpret the scores afterward.

"The functions of standardized tests are many and varied; however . . . they should help in decision-making," wrote education specialists Mehrens and Lehmann.[1] School officials use test scores to make decisions about what to teach students, and how well students are being taught. They look at scores to indicate what the school's strengths and weaknesses are.

Each standardized test must be written carefully. Each question tests a student's abilities or knowledge in very specific areas. For example, to develop a test in math, the developers must know which concepts are important to the school district asking for the test. Will it include adding fractions? Multiplication? What grade of students will be taking the test? What should be expected of those students?

This is a difficult and complex process because the items must reflect the curriculum. The questions must also be written so that they accurately reflect whether students who answer the items properly actually know the answer. For example, the correct answer to a poorly written question

Test Standards

The Standards for Educational and Psychological Testing were created by the American Educational Research Association, the American Psychological Association, and the National Council on Measurement in Education.

The standards include three categories:
• test construction, evaluation, and documentation
• fairness in testing
• testing applications (uses)

The standards are basic instructions for how to write a test that is valid, reliable, and fair to all the students who might take it.

may be obvious, even to students who do not know the subject. Author James Wardrop writes, "The items go through several cycles of editing, rewriting, and review before they are actually tried out."[2]

RELIABILITY

Reliability is an important aspect of a good test. Reliability has to do with consistency. This means that if a test is conducted repeatedly, the results of that test will be similar each time, even if the conditions are slightly different. This does not mean that all schools would score the same on a test that was reliable. But it does mean that schools would score the same way each time. A high-scoring school would get high scores each time the test was taken. A low-scoring school would get low scores each time.

For standardized tests, the conditions must be consistent.

Principles of Fairness in Testing

The *Standards for Educational and Psychological Testing* includes principles that help keep tests fair and prevent unintended consequences of testing:

• A single test should never be the only factor used for a decision about a student's education.

• The authority that mandates a test should describe how the results will be used and watch for negative consequences.

• If students do not speak English well or have a disability, test data has to be interpreted fairly and it may be necessary to make special arrangements for those students when they take the test.

Students get the same amount of time to finish the test, the same instructions, and the same questions to answer.

One way to test for reliability is to test a group of students, then test them again later and compare the two sets of scores. If the scores are similar, the test is more likely to be reliable. If they are different, test developers will look at the test again to find out why the test is not reliable.

But even if a test is reliable, many outside factors can affect a student's score. For example, if the test proctor gives one group of students more time to finish the tests, the scores can change. Students may not be

What Affects Test Performance?

Tests are intended to measure student knowledge. But knowledge is not all that affects a student's score. There are several other factors that can cause one student to do better, or worse, than another.

- **Test-wiseness**: Some students are simply better at taking tests than others. They are better at managing the time they have to take the test, guessing intelligently, and eliminating the wrong answers in multiple-choice questions.
- **Test anxiety**: Some students have more anxiety than others when taking a test or before taking a text. That anxiety can cause them to do badly on the test.
- **Language skills**: Any student whose first language is not English may be at a disadvantage compared to native English speakers.
- **Disabilities**: Students with dyslexia or other disabilities will not do as well as others on tests.
- **Poverty**: Students from low-income families are less likely to get extra help or coaching, especially from paid tutors.

motivated or be feeling well when they take the test. These and other factors can affect students' scores.

Validity

Validity is even more important than reliability. Validity is how accurately the test measures what it is supposed to measure. A test may show the same results consistently, but if it is not accurately measuring what it is supposed to, it is not a good test. For example, students who are good readers may do well on a math test because they are better able to understand the wording or the questions than other students. Their performance on the test would not be a good measure of their math ability.

For administrators to make judgments based on the test results, a test must be valid. Only scores on a valid test can help administrators understand students' abilities.

There are two types of validity in educational tests: content validity and criterion-related validity. Content validity means that the questions are valid in relation to the responses, or student's answers. That is, administrators can trust that if a student has the correct answer to a multiplication question, then that student knows how to multiply. Administrators would not be able to trust the validity of a test in which the answers were obvious even to students who did not know the multiplication tables.

Criterion-related validity means the students' test scores reflect their ability to actually perform the skill they are being tested on.

Sources of Error in Testing

Errors in test construction are a common type of error. For example, the test makers could mistakenly designate a wrong answer as a correct one. A question might also have more than one correct answer listed, though only one of those answers is designated as correct. A student might not get credit even if his or her answer was technically correct.

Errors such as these have occurred in the past. For example, in 2001, 45 percent of the 38 publicly released items on the Arizona Instrument to Measure Standards (AIMS) test were found to have errors. The questions were either incorrectly coded (wrong answers were selected by test makers as correct ones) or otherwise wrongly constructed.

Even if a test is free of errors, if it is used for purposes for which it was not designed, errors will happen. For example, the Iowa Tests of Basic Skills is used to help teachers adjust their instruction based on the skill levels of their students. But it is not intended to determine whether a student is ready for school enrollment, or whether to promote a student to the next grade level.

Test-Reporting Errors

Another type of error that can occur with standardized testing is test-reporting errors. Errors in test reporting occur when a test is not graded correctly. A student could lose credit despite answering a question accurately.

In 2002, test company Pearson made mistakes in grading 8,000 tests that determined whether high school seniors in Minnesota would graduate. The errors were caused by poor quality control. Excess moisture caused the test papers to expand before they were scanned. The error prevented hundreds of the seniors from graduating that year.

Tests that contain essay questions have to be scored by individual people. These scorers are often

Truth-in-Testing Laws

Truth-in-testing laws first passed in New York in 1979. Legislators passed laws that required testing companies to provide questions, answers, and information about how the tests are scored and their results analyzed. Since those laws passed, several cases in which large-scale errors affected numerous test takers have been reported in the news.

overworked. They may make errors in scoring an essay question, especially if the answer is written sloppily.

STUDENT ERROR

Another common type of error is student error. Students who take tests do not always fill in their answer sheets correctly. For example, if they fill out an answer on the wrong line, the rest of the test answers will be wrong because they are off by a line. This kind of error is difficult to prevent, but it is very common. The results of a test that contains errors such as these do not reflect a student's knowledge. ⌐

*Test scores at Monroe Elementary School rose on national achievement
tests after the school began offering after-school help.*

Schools in Camden, New Jersey, prepare students for the state's annual exam.

How Testing Affects Teaching

Standardized testing has been a part of education for decades. Students are tested repeatedly throughout elementary, middle, and high school. They take even more tests if they want to go to college.

Chapter 7

Educators, school officials, and lawmakers argue about the impact that standardized testing has on education. Depending on their points of view, standardized testing either improves or undermines education.

Both opponents and supporters of standardized testing in schools have research to back their positions. Studies that compare student scores to other types of outcomes (such as grade point averages) help determine whether there is a relationship between the two. Surveys of teachers who have administered standardized tests help show the impact of those tests on the classroom. Comparisons of students' scores on annual assessments can show whether students are learning more from year to year. Testing certainly has an impact on teaching and education, but is that impact good or bad?

Technology to the Rescue

One man has proposed a computer-based solution to testing issues. George Elford worked at Educational Testing Services (ETS) for 20 years. His solution to the testing dilemma is to create a computer system. He calls it an instructional management information system. The system could link teachers, classrooms, and databases. Teachers could record their judgments about how to improve students' performances.

Elford describes the drawbacks of standardized testing: "The practical answer is not to attack standardized testing."[1] The real answer, according to Elford, is to use the information gained from testing effectively.

In Favor: Accountability

Proponents of standardized testing, especially those in favor of the No Child Left Behind (NCLB) Act, support testing students and attaching consequences to the results. In doing so, they say schools are made accountable for how well they teach students.

Test results can help show what is working and what is not. "Test results can pinpoint a student's academic strengths and weaknesses," writes education author Richard Phelps.[2] If students do poorly on tests, the scores may be analyzed to determine how instruction should be changed. With the information gathered from standardized tests, proponents believe that schools can be improved, and students can receive a better education. Once the problem areas in a school are identified, schools are then responsible for instituting those changes and improving test scores.

In Favor: Motivating Students and Teachers

When students know that they will have to take a test, according to some psychologists, they are more likely to be motivated to learn. When they know that consequences will result from failure, they are also more likely to be motivated. Consequences could include such things as being held back a grade, not graduating, or not getting into college.

Some school districts offer teachers bonuses when their students show improved test scores. In the Quakertown Community School District, teachers get an incentive bonus when students succeed on tests.

Opposed: Testing Determines Curriculum

Sometimes, when test scores become a priority at a school, the

Proposed Changes to NCLB

For most educators, parents, and children today, standardized testing means NCLB. The National Education Association (NEA) has proposed some changes to this law, which, since 2007, can be reauthorized. NEA believes that these changes will improve NCLB:

- Use more than test scores to measure student learning and school performance.
- Include multiple measures of student learning and school effectiveness instead of just standardized tests.
- Reward progress over time to improve student achievement at all levels.
- Recognize individual needs of students (Special Education; English Language Learners).
- Reduce class size to help students learn.
- Restore the class size reduction program.
- Increase the number of highly qualified teachers in our schools.
- Provide financial incentives to teachers who teach in difficult-to-staff schools.
- Consider teachers who have achieved certification by the National Board for Professional Teaching Standards to be "highly qualified."
- Provide flexibility for teachers of multiple subjects, including special education and rural educators.

subject matter of the test will become a large part of the curriculum. This is also referred to as "teaching to the test." Teachers will change what they teach to give their students the best chance of doing well on tests. This helps raise test scores, but subjects that are not on the tests may be neglected or dropped from the curriculum entirely.

According to the authors of *The Unintended Consequences of High-Stakes Testing*:

> The downside of high-stakes testing in only a few subjects is the dramatic impact the policy has on nontested subjects. In our study of North Carolina elementary teachers' views of the impact of high-stakes testing, teachers reported that after the implementation of the testing program, they spent substantially more time teaching the tested subjects of mathematics, reading, and writing and less time teaching science, social studies, the arts, and physical education and health.[3]

OPPOSED: STUDENTS' SCORES ARE NOT A GOOD WAY TO JUDGE SCHOOLS

All students learn differently. Some students are motivated to learn simply because they find pleasure in doing so. Other students are motivated because of

*Parents of students at Scarsdale Middle School in New York protested
standardized testing because it takes time away from curriculum.*

rewards they will receive, or to avoid punishments.
Many educators do not believe that tests motivate all
students. Therefore, high-stakes tests might motivate
some students but decrease motivation in other
students.

High-stakes tests are used to determine whether
students will graduate, move up a grade, and get
academic honors. With such important rewards
or punishments at stake, it is important that all
students get a fair chance to earn or avoid them.
But what if the tests are unfair to certain groups, as

some research suggests? As stated in *The Unintended Consequences of High-Stakes Testing*, "minorities and students with disabilities tend to fail at higher rates than other students . . ."[4]

Under the Individuals with Disabilities Education Act, students with disabilities must have Individualized Education Plans (IEPs) that are created by parents, teachers, and other school officials. These plans give the student the resources to get a quality education despite his or her disability. This might include giving the student extra time to complete a test. But the existence of special conditions for some test takers raises questions about the data from a standardized test. If some test takers are experiencing different conditions than others while taking the test, the data from the scores can be called into question.

OPPOSED: LOWER STANDARDS

The consequences of standardized testing vary. When schools suffer large consequences for lower test scores, they have two options. They can either take actions to improve their scores, or they can lower the standards so that the scores meet the new goals.

In 2003, when the requirements of NCLB meant that some schools in Texas would be penalized, the State Board of Education found a way to avoid those penalties. It changed the rules. In an Associated Press story, reporter April Castro wrote, "Texas' standardized tests are not as difficult to pass as assessments in other states, a phenomenon that has created a false sense of success in the state that served as the model for President Bush's No Child Left Behind law."[5] Texas officials do not agree with the benchmarks that suggest the Texas exam is easier than other tests.

While NCLB allows states to choose their own standards, this aspect of testing is troublesome. Standardized test results can be helpful in diagnosing how to better teach students, but if states change standards rather than deal with test results, those students will not get the instruction they need.

Changes Already Made to NCLB

Some changes to NCLB have already been made. The U.S. Department of Education announced several changes between 2003 and 2006, including:
• Alternate or modified achievement standards for students with cognitive disabilities
• Exemption from state tests for students who have been in the country for less than a year
• More time and leeway for teachers to meet the act's "highly qualified" standards
• More options in the rule that 95 percent of students must take part in the state test

What Is Next?

NCLB mandates standardized testing in many grades and subjects. But even before NCLB passed, many states already had standardized testing programs in place. Both proponents and opponents of standardized testing are vocal about how they think tests should be used, and how testing programs should be changed. Until strong evidence emerges that tests are either harmful or helpful with student performance, the debate over how tests should be used will continue. ⌒

Teacher Leslie Sadler gave her students
practice tests to prepare for the state exam.

When students cheat on exams, the scores are unreliable.

CHEATING:
STUDENTS AND TEACHERS

For any test, cheating is an issue. Cheating is a fairly common practice. A 2006 study showed that 60 percent of high school students admitted that they had cheated on a classroom test at least once, and 35 percent said that they had done so more than once. Students cheat for a variety of reasons. Students who cheat have an unfair advantage over other, noncheating students.

With standardized tests, the issue is a little different. On many of these tests, students never see their scores. In addition, the scores do not make a difference in any grade for any class. Still, even in these cases, some students try to cheat.

However, not all standardized tests are low-stakes. In some states, such as Louisiana and Georgia, students must pass a standardized test in order to be promoted to the next grade. In Minnesota, students must pass the state test to graduate from high school. Stakes like those can lead students to cheat.

Because of student cheating, test results are not always accurate. This makes it difficult to make sure that the test scores reflect students' knowledge and abilities.

Overdoing Security?

Teachers and other test proctors generally follow strict procedures while standardized tests are going on. By monitoring the students as they take the tests, requiring them to turn off their cell phones, or taking away anything that might be used to cheat, test administrators help prevent cheating. Many standardized tests require that students remain in the classroom the entire duration of the test. But a *USA Today* article showed that sometimes test administrators go a little too far. "In late April, a sixth-grader in Ohio wet his pants during a standardized test after a teacher refused to let him use the bathroom," the article reported.[1]

But in standardized tests, students are not the only ones who might cheat. Sometimes, teachers and administrators have more to gain from test scores than the students do. In some cases, the educators have been caught cheating.

WHY WOULD TEACHERS CHEAT?

The idea that a teacher would cheat on a standardized test might sound strange. After all, it is the teachers who are usually monitoring to make sure that their students do not cheat. But there are actually several reasons why teachers might cheat.

A national survey of teachers, conducted by the National Board on Educational Testing and Public Policy in 2003, showed that small but significant percentages of teachers had engaged in what the board considered to be cheating during standardized tests.

Examples of Cheating

New Jersey began an investigation in 2005 of Camden schools. Allegations of cheating had been reported in the *Philadelphia Inquirer*. The state wanted to find out if these allegations were true. The state began to monitor tests conducted in Camden. After monitoring began, students' average scores dropped by 70 percentage points.

Nearly 700 schools in Texas were investigated after a testing security company analyzed the scores on the state test. The company found that many schools had unexplained changes in average scores. It also found answer sheets that seemed to have been copied or altered after the test.

[A]bout 10 percent of the teachers admitted to providing hints about the answers during the test administration; about 10 percent pointed out mismarked items by students; about 15 percent of the teachers provided more time for the test than was allowed; and about 5 percent of the teachers engaged in instruction during the test.[2]

The reasons that teachers cheat are often related to what is at stake in the test. If a student fails the test it could mean he or she may not graduate or move up a grade. Teachers care about their students and what happens to them. The cheating they engage in is often done with the best of intentions.

But some cheating is done with selfish intentions. Occasionally, teachers are offered bonuses for improving the test scores of their students. Their job-performance ratings may be affected by test scores. No Child Left Behind (NCLB) requires that test scores improve each year or schools could lose federal funding. Schools in need of that funding may put pressure on teachers to make sure the scores improve. In order to achieve higher scores, some teachers may resort to cheating.

According to education researchers Sharon Nichols and David Berliner:

Many of the teachers who admit to cheating or who have been found doing so have as their motive a desire for their students to do well on the tests. . . . But whether such teacher behavior is judged to be either noble or ignoble . . . the result is exactly the same. Cheating of whatever kind decreases the validity of the tests and adds uncertainty to whatever decisions are made on the basis of the test scores.[3]

How Do They Cheat?

There are many ways for teachers to cheat on a test. One way is to distribute copies of the test to students. "This is what happened in Nevada, where two high school teachers allegedly copied test questions and handed them out to students to use as a study guide," Nichols and Berliner wrote in their book *Collateral Damage*.[4] Nichols and Berliner also cite other incidents in Massachusetts, North Carolina, and California, when teachers either confessed to or were accused of giving out the test questions before the actual test.

Test Security Audits

Some states use a test security company to audit their testing program. In a test security audit, representatives of the company visit on-site to meet the people who manage and develop the testing program.

They ask questions about how tests are kept secure. They ask about how testing is conducted. They review nondisclosure agreements. They may also ask how tests were developed, or how scores were validated.

Another form of cheating is when teachers coach students during tests. Cheating teachers may point out wrong answers or simply tell students what the correct answers are. Teachers may do this for many reasons, such as concern for their students, the school's status based on the resulting test scores, or their personal opposition to standardized testing. According to Nichols and Berliner, "When students are asked to collaborate in cheating, it is especially worrisome. It may be the reason some believe we are developing a culture that condones and justifies instances of cheating."[5]

Even if teachers do not engage in this kind of cheating before or during the test, there are still opportunities for cheating. After the tests have finished, teachers and other staff at the school could alter the tests. Because standardized tests are mostly multiple-choice questions, teachers may simply fill in random answers to any unanswered questions. Blank answers would be marked as incorrect by the testing company. By filling in the blanks on an answer sheet, there is a good chance the student's test will have a few more correct answers.

Another way that teachers have cheated is by changing the students' answers on their completed answer sheets. On many standardized tests, the most difficult questions are at the end of a section. These questions are most likely to have wrong answers. Once the test is finished, a cheating teacher could erase the last few answers on each answer sheet and fill in the correct answers.

PREVENTING CHEATING

Teachers have been caught cheating and stopped, sometimes by the students themselves. Researchers Nichols and Berliner wrote, "In Pennsylvania, a fourth-grade student complained to his mother that

How Schools and Districts Prevent Cheating

Cheating is bad publicity for schools. Cheating means that the test was not valid. Administrators need accurate results from the standardized tests so they can monitor the school's progress. Some ways that schools and districts work to prevent cheating are as follows:

- Teachers and other school personnel are not allowed to see test questions until the day of the test.
- Test booklets are individually shrink-wrapped.
- Volunteer test proctors, who do not have a stake in the test scores, monitor the test instead of teachers or principals.
- Answer sheets are examined by the testing company for evidence of tampering.
- State monitoring teams occasionally visit testing sites unannounced to make sure that proper test procedures are being followed.
- Specific policies for test security are distributed so that teachers know what is okay and what is prohibited, both for test preparation and for proctoring the test.

The Texas Education Agency announced that it planned to improve security measures for the state's standardized tests.

he was tired of tests and tired of his teacher putting Post-it notes on his exam telling him to go back and revisit answers that are 'wrong.'"[6] Testing companies have also developed computer programs to analyze data and detect patterns that indicate that a teacher might be cheating. One Utah company named Caveon specializes in test security and detection of test fraud.

But short of watching every teacher involved in standardized testing at every moment, there is no way to make it impossible for cheating to take place. Some opponents of high-stakes standardized tests such as the ones required by NCLB believe that cheating is inevitable when so much emphasis is placed on the tests. According to education researchers Nichols and Berliner:

> *Educators, like almost everyone else, are tempted to make improper decisions when there is exaggerated emphasis on a single indicator and their jobs or their students' futures are at stake. We believe that teachers are now no less or more moral than they ever have been. Instead, what we believe is that teachers have been placed by our politicians in untenable positions, environments where pressures encourage questionable behavior.*[7]

*Some teachers have been caught changing
answers on students' exams.*

Test scores can affect school funding. For example, a school might have less money to spend on technology and books if tests scores are low.

CHEATING:
STATES AND DISTRICTS

heating on standardized tests sometimes goes beyond classroom cheating by students and teachers. When test scores could have consequences for the school system, even districts and states have been known to cheat.

What reason could the state as a whole have for cheating? That depends on what the consequences are for low scores. The Elementary and Secondary Education Act was revised in 1994. It required schools to improve their graduation standards and test scores in order to receive federal funding. Test scores became much more important than they ever had been before. Without federal funding, schools would have less money for new textbooks, teachers' salaries, or computer equipment. As a result, a school in which test scores drop might face cutbacks or parent outrage at lost funding.

With funding on the line, school officials might be tempted to artificially improve students' scores to make the scores look better than they are.

CAMPBELL'S LAW

In 1975, a sociologist named Donald Campbell put forth his Campbell's law. It states that if one indicator is used too heavily in decision making, that indicator is likely to become corrupt. In other words, "The higher the stakes, the more likely people are to cheat."[1]

Those who oppose the tests mandated by No Child Left Behind (NCLB) often cite Campbell's law. They suggest that if scores from standardized tests are used to determine a school's fate, those schools and districts are likely to become corrupted.

Education researchers Sharon Nichols and John Berliner wrote:

Serious, life-altering decisions that affect teachers, administrators, and students are made on the basis of testing. Tests determine who is promoted and who is retained. Tests can determine who will receive a high school degree and who will not. Test scores can determine if a school will be reconstituted, if there will be job

Reporting NCLB Data

One provision of NCLB says that when states report on test results, they have to provide separate reports for certain subgroups. These groups include:

- economically disadvantaged students
- students with disabilities
- students with limited English proficiency (LEP)
- major racial and ethnic groups
- gender

In the past, schools or districts sometimes distorted their test data by leaving out certain groups. For example, if students with disabilities did poorly on the tests, they might be excluded from the test. Sometimes, as in the case of Tennessee in 2003, students whose academic performances were weak were not allowed to take the tests so that their scores would not bring down the school's average. "Weak students were seen herded to the school library to watch movies for a week while academically stronger students took exams," report education researchers Nichols and Berliner.[2]

Testing under NCLB attempts to ensure that students are not excluded from testing. NCLB requires 95 percent of a school's students to participate in the tests. In addition, schools are required to report the scores of certain populations of students such as ESL students and students with disabilities.

losses for teachers and administrators when scores do not improve, or if there will be cash bonuses when scores do improve.[3]

According to Nichols and Berliner, if this much emphasis is placed on test scores, test scores will inevitably become corrupt through cheating.

How They Cheat

Educators disagree about whether cheating is inevitable. But there is no doubt that cheating happens. Districts or states are sometimes inclined to make the scores look better when students do not do well on tests.

Some schools will prevent students from taking the test if those students are not expected to do well. In 2005, a nonprofit organization called Advocates for Children filed a lawsuit against the Boys and Girls High School in Brooklyn, New York. They said that the high school had forced students out of the school. The school had kept students out of classes and then informed those students that they did not have enough credits to graduate. According to an article in the *New York Times*:

By pushing out students who are failing and unlikely to graduate, . . . schools can raise their test-score averages and graduation rates while reducing suspensions and dropout rates. In response to earlier cases, the city adopted new discharge codes . . . to improve tracking of the reasons students leave high school, and it settled two federal lawsuits by promising to readmit students who were forced out without diplomas.[4]

NCLB requires each state to report the standardized test scores of students in its schools. They must also report graduation rates. This is an opportunity to cheat. Schools or districts may not accurately report the graduation rates. They may also adjust the numbers so that graduation rates appear higher.

One example comes from Massachusetts. Education researchers Nichols and Berliner report:

[T]he state claimed that 96 percent of the class of 2004 had passed the MCAS and thus would graduate high school. What the state failed to disclose, however, was the dropout rate. The class of 2004 had lost 18,232 students from grades 9–12. That represents a 23 percent dropout rate and makes the actual passing rate of the 2004 graduating class 74 percent, not 96 percent.[5]

Not all schools, districts, or states participate in this kind of dishonesty. Some discrepancies may be simple mistakes rather than intentional deception. However, any form of cheating makes test scores less reliable. Cheating could mean that decisions are being made based on flawed data.

The Old-fashioned Way

Some districts and states improve their scores by improving instruction. They drill students in the subjects covered on the tests and get parents involved.

"Tests can provide useful feedback on teaching and learning when they are developed and used properly. Tests can also lead to serious, if unintended negative consequences for students, educators, and schools. Because tests can have such positive or negative consequences, it is important to monitor their use in an ongoing fashion."[6]
—*The National Board on Educational Testing and Public Policy*

In the Pajaro Valley Unified School District, in Watsonville, California, scores on standardized math tests went up among students who participated in after-school programs. These students' math scores were more than 2.5 times better than the state average. Their reading scores improved as well.

The programs, which were not mandatory, combined academic tutoring with recreational activities such as swim lessons at the local YMCA. Students who participated spent as much as three extra hours at school.

In Michigan, schools in the Pontiac School
District used state grants to fund educational
programs. The district started gifted and talented,
bilingual, and early childhood education programs.
With a federal grant, the district started technology,
literacy, and after-school programs.

In Pontiac, elementary students' math scores
increased by 23 percent between 2003 and 2004.
Math scores in the middle school increased by
20 percent. Both of these were far above the state
average scores. In other areas, such as English-
language arts and social studies, Pontiac middle
school students' scores increased while state averages
dropped. ⌐

Test scores improved at Marlin Elementary School in Texas.

The Texas Public Education Reform Foundation reported that
64 percent of Texans favor standardized testing in schools.

PUBLIC OPINION

Standardized testing has only gotten more
attention since the passage of No Child
Left Behind (NCLB). Public opinion about the act
and standardized testing is mixed. Many people have
strong opinions about it.

Consider the story of Scarsdale, New York. In 2001, parents and teachers protested against standardized tests. Students' test scores in the suburb were the highest in the nation, but parents and teachers opposed the use of standardized tests. "School board members and the local PTA have made repeated public statements opposing the tests," wrote *New York Times* reporter Kate Zernike. "Parents [of eighth graders] . . . have pledged to keep their children home from school when the tests are administered."[1]

Teachers, parents, and school officials believed that the tests were causing harm to students. All the test preparation "stifled creativity and forced teachers to abandon the very programs that have made the schools excel."[2] Only 95 out of 290 students of the eighth grade class took the test that year. The boycott attracted media attention and prompted others to express their agreement. This boycott took place before NCLB began requiring more standardized testing nationwide.

FUNDING SCHOOLS BASED ON TEST SCORES

Many efforts have been made over the years to determine what the public really thinks about standardized testing. However, most polls on this have been local rather than national.

In 2006, the well-known polling organization Zogby conducted a poll for the *Miami Herald.* The people who responded were asked whether they agreed with grading and funding schools based on their test scores. Sixty-one percent of respondents did not support grading and funding schools based on test scores.

What Makes a Good Poll?

Polls are a good way to gauge people's opinions. But not all polls are the same. The most credible polls include the answers to these questions somewhere in the report of the findings.

- *How big was the sample?* The sample is the number of people who were asked about the polled topic. Generally, the bigger the sample, the better the poll.
- *What was the exact question asked?* Questions for polls should be written to avoid bias. That means that the question must not suggest an answer.
- *Who conducted the poll?* Polling organizations are usually the most reliable because they are well versed in asking unbiased questions and finding good samples of respondents. For example, Gallup and Zogby are well-known and established pollsters.

EMPHASIS ON TESTING

Another poll in Texas also suggested some opposition to standardized testing. Respondents to the Texas poll did not support the way that testing affects education. The Texas State Teachers Association conducted a poll in February of 2007. They asked respondents what they thought about the emphasis on testing in Texas schools. Twenty-six percent of respondents said testing was emphasized the right amount, while 60 percent said it was emphasized too much.

Despite this opposition, the respondents wanted to change, not eliminate, the standardized testing program. They wanted tests to be used to diagnose students' strengths and weaknesses "rather than triggering serious penalties for schools and students."[3] They also felt that classroom performance and grades should be more important in determining advancement and graduation. They wanted to "allow more school time to be devoted to learning instead of teaching to the test."[4]

LINKING TEACHER PAY TO TEST SCORES

Some have suggested the possibility of linking teacher pay to test scores. Louis Gerstner, the former CEO of IBM, formed a group called the Teaching Commission in 2003. In 2005, the group did some polling to find out whether the public would support the commission's ideas about increasing teacher salaries. The commission wanted to link teachers'

Parents of students at the Brooklyn Free School did not support strict curricula or standardized tests.

pay to their students' test scores. The nationwide polling found that 41 percent of respondents wanted to link teachers' pay to test scores. However, 52 percent of respondents did not feel that standardized tests accurately measure student achievement. Of the teachers who responded to the poll, only 13 percent supported the idea.

Opinions of NCLB

Public opinion on standardized testing is divided. While some support its use in certain situations, others feel testing is an interruption in the classroom environment. This is truer than ever since the passage of NCLB. This legislation is about more than standardized testing. But for many, because NCLB requires so much standardized testing, the two are the same. Public opinion about NCLB is sharply divided.

The Center on Education Policy released a study on test scores since NCLB passed in 2001. It said that the gaps in test scores between white students and Hispanic and African-American students had narrowed since the law was passed. But the organization "warned repeatedly against concluding that the federal law alone produced the results."[5]

Other studies have suggested that the law has had negative results. A 2006 report from Education Sector, a Washington DC think tank for education policy, said that the testing sector is struggling with the demands of reform plans. The testing sector has faced increased demand for new and frequent tests in every state.

In 2003, a nationwide poll found that 78 percent of public school parents knew very little or nothing at all about NCLB. In 2007, that number fell to 35 percent. Of those respondents who knew a great deal or a fair amount about NCLB, 55 percent had a somewhat unfavorable or a very unfavorable impression of the NCLB.

Based on previous years' data, the study showed declining levels of support for NCLB. "It seems fair to say that . . . the public's view of NCLB is growing less and less favorable," the study concluded.[6]

But respondents were also asked whether the increase in testing in the last decade had helped, hurt, or made no difference in academic performance. Parents of public school children who answered the survey were almost evenly divided: 32 percent said it had helped, 32 percent said it had hurt, and 35 percent said it had made no difference.

With an issue as complex as standardized testing, it is unlikely that there will ever be full agreement on its proper uses or its fairness. But the argument will continue to drive public policy and influence how testing is used.

Mitchell and Judy Stiers of Cedar Falls, Iowa, are confident that
local schools will meet the new standards set by NCLB.

TIMELINE

2200 BCE	1000	1905
First use of standardized testing exists in China.	Early universities begin to require students to pass tests to earn advanced degrees.	Psychologist Alfred Binet and Theodore Simon create a test to determine whether schoolchildren need more help in school.

1936	1947
IBM demonstrates a new machine that can automatically score standardized tests.	The Educational Testing Service (ETS) is formed to administer the SAT.

1906

Lewis Terman revises the Binet-Simon scale to create the Stanford-Binet IQ test.

1917

The U.S. Army creates its Army Alpha Test and administers it to literate soldiers throughout World War I.

1926

Professor Carl Brigham updates and revises the Army Alpha Test, creating the Scholastic Assessment Test (SAT).

1959

American College Testing nonprofit agency is formed and begins to administer the American College Test (ACT).

1965

Elementary and Secondary Education Act (ESEA) passes Congress and begins to federally fund schools.

TIMELINE

1989

President George
H. W. Bush convenes
the nation's governors
at a conference to
come up with higher
academic standards.

1994

Congress renews
ESEA and adds
encouragement
to meet higher
academic standards.

2002

President George W.
Bush signs NCLB into
law on January 8.

2005

Schools begin
administering tests
under NCLB for
reading and math.

2001

No Child Left Behind
Act (NCLB) passes
on May 23.

2001

NCLB passes the
Senate on June 14.

2007

Schools begin
administering tests
under NCLB
in science.

2007

Legislation is
proposed to
change NCLB.

ESSENTIAL FACTS

AT ISSUE

Opposed

❖ Standardized testing takes away from time in the classroom.

❖ Testing is not a good way to measure all students' abilities.

❖ States sometimes cheat in reporting test results on standardized tests.

❖ Testing puts unfair demands on students and teachers.

In Favor

❖ Testing helps government agencies monitor a school's progress.

❖ Standardized test scores help administrators identify problems in a school, and curriculum can be changed to address the needs of the students.

❖ Standardized testing holds teachers and schools accountable.

❖ Testing may help motivate students and teachers.

CRITICAL DATES

1950s
Americans began to be concerned about the state of public education. Among other reasons, it seemed that the nation's chief adversary, the Soviet Union, was outdoing the United States in science and in education.

1965
The Elementary and Secondary Education Act established that schools would get federal as well as local funding if they met certain conditions.

1980s
Concern reached a peak, and the conditions for standardized testing became ripe.

1994
The Elementary and Secondary Education Act of 1965 was renewed with more focus on testing in certain grades.

2002
The No Child Left Behind Act passed in 2001 and was signed into law by President George W. Bush in 2002. It mandated more standardized testing for public schoolchildren, and required schools to meet yearly progress goals or be designated as "failing" schools.

2007
Legislation was introduced to make significant changes to No Child Left Behind.

QUOTES

"The downside of high-stakes testing in only a few subjects is the dramatic impact the policy has on nontested subjects. . . . Teachers reported that after the implementation of the testing program, they spent substantially more time teaching the tested subjects of mathematics, reading, and writing and less time teaching science, social studies, the arts, and physical education and health."— *M. Gail Jones, Brett Jones, and Tracy Hargrove*

"Today, pressed by the federal No Child Left Behind Act, states, districts and schools are being held more accountable for their actual academic performance. Though there is much debate over how results should be measured—whether with traditional standardized tests, or more subjective portfolio assessments—there is widening agreement that education reform should focus on student achievement." — *Thomas B. Fordham Foundation*

ADDITIONAL RESOURCES

SELECT BIBLIOGRAPHY

Chubb, John (ed.) *Within Our Reach: How America Can Educate Every Child.* Lanham, MD: Rowman & Littlefield Publishers, 2005.

Harris, Joseph. *What Every Parent Needs to Know About Standardized Tests: How to Understand the Tests and Help Your Kids Score High!* New York: McGraw-Hill, 2002.

Jones, M. Gail, Brett Jones, and Tracy Hargrove. *The Unintended Consequences of High-Stakes Testing.* Lanham, MD: Rowman & Littlefield Publishers, 2003.

Mehrens, William A., and Irvin J. Lehmann. *Using Standardized Tests in Education*, 4th ed. New York: Longman Inc., 1987.

National Center for Fair and Open Testing. "What's Wrong With Standardized Tests?" Fairtest.org, 17 Dec. 2007. 13 Feb. 2008 <http://www.fairtest.org/whats-wrong-standardized-tests>.

Phelps, Richard P. *Kill the Messenger: The War on Standardized Testing.* New Brunswick, NJ: Transaction Publishers, 2003.

FURTHER READING

Forte, Imogene, and Marjorie Frank. *Reading & Language: If You're Trying to Get Better Grades and Higher Test Scores, You've Gotta Have This Book!* Nashville, TN: Incentive Publications, 2003.

Henningfeld, Diane Andrews. *Standardized Testing.* Detroit: Greenhaven Press, 2007.

Soper, Marty. *Crash Course for Study Skills: Setting Goals, Managing Time, Listening, Taking Notes, Studying, Taking Tests, Learning Attitude, Learning Style.* East Moline, IL: LinguiSystems, 1995.

Web Links

To learn more about standardized testing in schools, visit ABDO Publishing Company on the World Wide Web at **www.abdopublishing.com**. Web sites about standardized testing in schools are featured on our Book Links page. These links are routinely monitored and updated to provide the most current information available.

For More Information

For more information on this subject, contact or visit the following organizations.

Educational Testing Services (ETS)
Rosedale Road, Princeton, NJ 08541
609-921-9000
www.ets.org
ETS provides educators with assessments and research to advance the quality of education.

The National Center for Fair & Open Testing (FairTest)
342 Broadway, Cambridge, MA 02139
617-864-4810
www.fairtest.org/about
FairTest works to eliminate the misuse of and flaws in standardized tests. It also seeks to end racial, class, and cultural bias in testing.

U.S. Department of Education
400 Maryland Avenue, SW, Washington DC 20202
800-872-5327
www.ed.gov
The U.S. Department of Education is a federal agency that works to promote student achievement and to provide equal opportunities in public schools.

GLOSSARY

accountability
The quality or state of being held responsible for something.

adequate yearly progress (AYP)
Annual goals that schools, districts, or states set for improvement of student test scores.

Campbell's law
A social science law that says that the more important something is, the more likely it will become corrupted.

competency
The ability to do something well.

criterion-referenced
A test that scores mastery of a skill set.

curriculum
Everything that is to be taught to students.

diagnostic test
A test intended to find out what a student's strengths and weaknesses in a subject area are.

failing (NCLB)
Under the No Child Left Behind Act, schools are labeled as "failing" if they do not make adequate yearly progress for two years in a row.

highly qualified (NCLB)
Under the No Child Left Behind Act, teachers are to be "highly qualified," which means that they have a bachelor's degree and substantive knowledge in the area they teach.

high-stakes testing
Testing in which there are some consequences associated with passing or failing a test for the test taker.

IQ
Intelligence quotient; a measure of how intelligent a person is.

mandated
Required.

norm-referenced
> A test in which scores are compared to a norm group.

percentile
> An expression of a norm-referenced score; a student who does better than 80 percent of the other students is in the eightieth percentile.

proctor
> Someone who monitors a test to prevent cheating, gives instructions, and answers questions.

reliability
> The degree to which a test administered in the same conditions gets close to the same results.

standardized test
> A test that everyone takes, with the same instructions, in the same conditions. It is usually created by a test publishing company.

standards-based education
> Education in which the curriculum taught to students is guided by clearly stated standards.

supplemental educational services
> Tutoring, coaching, or other kinds of academic help outside the classroom.

test anxiety
> A fear of taking tests.

test-wiseness
> Skills in taking tests well.

validity
> The degree to which a test actually measures what it is supposed to measure.

Source Notes

Chapter 1. No Child Left Behind

1. United States Congress, "No Child Left Behind Act of 2001." Public Law 107–110, 115 Stat. 1425, Sec. 1001, 8 Jan. 2002. 2 Jun. 2008 <ed.gov/policy/elsec/leg/esea02/pg1.html>.
2. Ibid.
3. W. James Popham. *America's "Failing" Schools: How Parents and Teachers Can Cope With No Child Left Behind*. New York: Routledge Falmer, 2004. 22.

Chapter 2. Testing Controversy

1. Progressive Policy Institute. "And High School Reform, Too." 21st Century Schools Project Bulletin, Vol. 5, no. 1. 11 Jan. 2005. Washington DC: Progressive Policy Institute. 13 Feb. 2008 <http://www.ppionline.org/ppi_ci.cfm?contentid=253108&knlgAreaID=110&subsecid=900001>.
2. National Center for Fair and Open Testing. "What's Wrong with Standardized Tests?" Fairtest.org, 17 Dec. 2007. 13 Feb. 2008 <http://www.fairtest.org/whats-wrong-standardized-tests>.
3. Ibid.
4. Thomas B. Fordham Foundation. "Testing and Accountability." Washington DC: Thomas B. Fordham Foundation. 13 Feb. 2008 <http://www.edexcellence.net/foundation/topic/topic.cfm?topic=Testing%20%26%20Accountability>.

Chapter 3. The History of Testing

1. James L. Wardrop. *Standardized Testing in the Schools: Uses and Roles*. Belmont, CA.: Wadsworth Publishing Company, 1976. 7.
2. J. A. Plucker (Ed.). (2003). *Human Intelligence: Historical Influences, Current Controversies, Teaching Resources*. 1 Feb. 2008 <http://www.indiana.edu/~intell/terman.shtml>.
3. National Commission on Excellence in Education. "A Nation at Risk." National Commission on Excellence in Education, 1983. 12 Mar. 2008 <http://www.ed.gov/pubs/NatAtRisk/index.html>.
4. John F. Jennings. *Why Nationals Standards and Tests? Politics and the Quest for Better Schools*. Thousand Oaks, CA.: Sage Publications, 1998. 5.
5. Ibid. 6.

6. U.S. Department of Education. *America 2000: An Education Strategy.*
Washington D.C.: U.S. Department of Education, 1991. 12 Feb.
2008 <http://www.eric.ed.gov/ERICDocs/data/ericdocs2sql/
content_storage_01/0000019b/80/22/b3/55.pdf>.
7. Ibid.

Chapter 4. Standards and Scoring
1. William Mehrens and Irvin Lehmann. *Using Standardized Tests in Education*, 4th ed. New York: Longman Inc., 1987. 105.
2. Nancy W. Sindelar. *Using Test Data for Student Achievement.* Lanham, MD: Rowman & Littlefield, 2006. 72.
3. William Mehrens and Irvin Lehmann. *Using Standardized Tests in Education*, 4th ed. New York: Longman Inc., 1987. 108.

Chapter 5. What Is a Standardized Test?
None

Chapter 6. Writing a Good Test
1. William A. Mehrens and Irvin J. Lehmann. *Using Standardized Tests in Education*, 4th ed. New York: Longman, 1987. 11.
2. James L. Wardrop. *Standardized Testing in the Schools.* Monterey, CA: Brooks/Cole Publishing Company, 1976. 73.

Chapter 7. How Testing Affects Teaching
1. George W. Elford. *Beyond Standardized Testing: Better Information for School Accountability and Management.* Lanham, MD: Scarecrow Press, 2002. xi.
2. Richard P. Phelps. *Kill the Messenger: The War on Standardized Testing.* New Brunswick, NJ: Transaction Publishers, 2003. 225.
3. M. Gail Jones, Brett D. Jones and Tracy Y. Hargrove. *The Unintended Consequences of High-Stakes Testing.* Lanham, MD: Rowman & Littlefield, 2003. 29.
4. Ibid. 109.
5. April Castro. "Is TAKS Too Easy?" October 4, 2007, Associated Press. 11 Mar. 2008 <http://www.kdhnews.com/news/story.aspx?id=19261&q=april+castro>.

Source Notes Continued

Chapter 8. Cheating: Students and Teachers
1. Jeffrey D. McDonald. "Teachers Can Say No When Students Have to Go." *USA Today*, 4 June 2007, Life Section. 6d. 2 Jun. 2008 <http://www.usatoday.com/news/education/2007-06-03-children-bathroom-breaks_N.htm>.
2. Sharon L. Nichols and David C. Berliner. *Collateral Damage: How High-Stakes Testing Corrupts America's Schools*. Cambridge, MA.: Harvard Education Press, 2007. 36.
3. Ibid. 37.
4. Ibid. 39.
5. Ibid. 40.
6. Ibid.
7. Ibid. 34.

Chapter 9. Cheating: States and Districts
1. Joshua Benton and Holly K. Hacker. "Efforts to stop TAKS cheating often fall short," *The Dallas Morning News.* 4 June 2007. 2 Jun. 2008 <http://www.dallasnews.com/sharedcontent/dws/dn/education/stories/060507dnmetsecurity.37550f3.html>.
2. Sharon Nichols and David Berliner. *Collateral Damage: How High-Stakes Testing Corrupts America's Schools*. Cambridge, MA: Harvard University Press, 2007. 36.
3. Ibid. 30.
4. David Herszenhorn. "Brooklyn High School Is Accused Anew of Forcing Students Out." *New York Times*, 12 Oct. 2005, Section B; Column 1.
5. Sharon Nichols and David Berliner. *Collateral Damage: How High-Stakes Testing Corrupts America's Schools.* Cambridge, MA: Harvard University Press, 2007. 85.
6. National Board on Educational Testing and Public Policy. "About the Board." Undated. 13 Feb. 2008 <http://www.bc.edu/research/nbetpp/about_general.html>.

Chapter 10. Public Opinion

1. Kate Zernike. "In High-Scoring Scarsdale, A Revolt Against Tests." *New York Times*, 13 Apr. 2001, Section A, Column 3. 1.

2. Ibid.

3. Texas State Teachers Association. "Voter Opinion on Education in the State of Texas." Austin, TX: Texas State Teachers Association, 6 Feb. 2007. 17 Feb. 2008 <http://www.tsta.org/news/current/pollsters0207.shtml>.

4. Ibid.

5. Sam Dillon. "New Study Finds Gains Since No Child Left Behind." *New York Times*, 6 June 2007, Section B, Column 1. 7.

6. Lowell C. Rose and Alec M. Gallup. "The 39th Annual Phi Delta Kappa/Gallup Poll of the Public's Attitudes Toward the Public Schools." Phi Delta Kappa International, 2007. 17 Feb. 2008 <http://www.pdkmembers.org/members_online/publications/e-GALLUP/kpoll_pdfs/pdkpoll39_2007.pdf>.

INDEX

ABOUT THE AUTHOR

Holly Dolezalek is a freelance writer who has been covering educational technology and training since 2002. She is based in Minneapolis, Minnesota, and writes for several magazines and newsletters, including *Training* magazine, where she was an editor on staff from 2002 to 2005.

PHOTO CREDITS

Eric Risberg/AP Images, cover; Marcy Nighswander/AP Images, 6; Ron Edmonds/AP Images, 9; Frederick Bass/Getty Images, 15; Seth Perlman/AP Images, 16; Benjamin Sklar/AP; Images, 20, 50; Carlos Osorio/AP Images, 23; Nina Leen/Time & Life Pictures / Getty Images, 24; Time & Life Pictures/Getty Images, 27; Doug Mills/AP Images, 33; Buzz Orr/AP Images, 34; Red Line Editorial, 38; Stefan Klein/iStock Images, 41; Rui Vieira/AP Images, 42; Pat Wellenbach/AP Images, 47; Charles Gupton/Corbis, 49; Charles Bennett/AP Images, 59; Brian Branch-Price/AP Images, 60, 69; Stephen Chernin/AP Images, 65; photos_alyson/Getty Images, 70; Harry Cabluck /AP Images, 77, 88; Superstudio/Getty Images, 79; John S. Stewart/AP Images, 80; Ron Aydelotte/AP Images, 87; Bebeto Matthews/AP Images, 92; Charlie Niebergall/AP Images, 95